STARTERS

SPACE

Written by
Nick Pierce

Illustrated by
Steve Wood

This edition published MMXIX by Scribblers,
an imprint of The Salariya Book Company Ltd
25 Marlborough Place,
Brighton BN1 1UB
www.salariya.com

© The Salariya Book Company Ltd MMXIX

PB ISBN-13: 978-1-912537-24-2

1 3 5 7 9 8 6 4 2

A CIP catalogue record for this book is available
from the British Library.

Printed and bound in China.

Printed on paper from sustainable sources.

Visit
www.salariya.com
for our online catalogue and
free fun stuff.

Consultant:
Dr Stuart Clark holds a first class honours
degree and a PhD in astrophysics. He is a
Fellow of the Royal Astronomical Society and a
former Vice Chair of the Association of British
Science Writers. He writes the Guardian's 'Across
the Universe' blog and articles for New Scientist,
and is the author of The Search for Earth's Twin.

Contents

Introduction   4

The solar system   6

Our home planet   8

Watching the sky   10

Moons   12

People on the Moon   14

Working in space   16

Space probes   18

Timeline   20

Quiz   22

Glossary   23

Index   24

Introduction

When you look up into the sky you are looking into space. The Earth's sunlit, day-time sky looks empty, but at night-time you can see thousands of objects that are millions of miles away. At such huge distances the stars look like tiny points of light, and even galaxies with billions of stars are only faint smudges to us on Earth. But up close, the view changes. Space is full of potato-shaped moons, exploding stars, giant balls of gas, city-sized dirty snowballs that are too small to be seen from Earth and much more.

On each spread you will have to look for different objects in the main picture.

The universe is everything: it's everything you can see, everything you can think of and much, much more. The universe contains you and the planet Earth where we all live. It includes the solar system, the family of planets of which Earth is part, and the Milky Way galaxy, the massive star system in which our solar system is found. At vast distances are many millions more galaxies, each one moving further apart as the universe keeps expanding.

Can you find...?

◀Asteroids
Asteroids are fragments of rock and metal. The asteroid Gaspra is about 12 kilometres (7.5 miles) across.

▲Jupiter
Jupiter is the giant of the solar system. It is more than 11 times wider than our planet, Earth. It is made mostly of gases and is known as a 'gas giant'.

▲Venus
Venus is the hottest and brightest planet in the solar system. It is surrounded by a poisonous atmosphere.

◀Mercury
Mercury is made of rock and is covered in craters. It is the closest planet to the Sun. It is scorching hot by day and freezing at night.

The solar system

The solar system is the Sun and its surrounding family of planets, moons, asteroids and comets. It was created out of a vast cloud of gas and dust. Most of the cloud's energy was used to create the Sun — the gigantic star at its centre. At the same time it formed the asteroids and comets, many of which came together to form the planets and their moons.

▲Comets
Beyond Pluto, there are billions of comets. These giant space 'snowballs' are made of ice, gases, rocks and dust.

▼The Sun
The Sun is a hot spinning ball of luminous gas called a star. It is the biggest object in the solar system. The Sun's gravity keeps its family of planets together in space.

▶Earth

Earth is unique. It is the only planet we know of with life. Around three-quarters of its surface is covered in water.

Can you find...?

▲Balloon

People have travelled in balloons into near-space. In 2014, Alan Eustace reached a height of 41.4 km (25.73 miles).

▲Satellite

Satellites orbiting the Earth can collect information about our weather systems. They can also identify mineral deposits, crops and movements of sea life.

▲Plane

Aircraft often fly in the stratosphere, the second layer of the Earth's atmosphere.

Our home planet

Earth is unique. It is the only planet that we know of with life. Water covers around three-quarters of its surface, and it is home to millions of different life forms. The gases that form the Earth's atmosphere keep its surface temperature warm enough to support life.

9

Watching the sky

▲Modern telescope

Telescopes based on Earth can look into space, as most light and radio waves get through Earth's atmosphere. Satellite telescopes reveal much more.

▲Constellations

Constellations are patterns of stars that have a recognisable shape, sometimes of an animal or mythical creature. People once used these constellations to navigate.

◄William Herschel (1738–1822)

Herschel was a British astronomer who built telescopes to study the stars. He discovered the planet Uranus in the process.

◀Fire
Can you find the fire in this picture?

▲Mayan
The Mayans were one of the earliest civilisations to study the movement of the stars before the invention of telescopes.

The first humans simply used their eyes to look up at the hundreds of stars in the night sky. Those they called 'wandering stars' we now know as the planets. Today we use computer-controlled telescopes. They are built high on mountaintops, away from city lights and above the clouds, to capture the clearest views. They look into space and record what they see for us.

▲Hipparchus
Hipparchus, considered the greatest astronomer of the ancient world, was Greek. He made some of the earliest accurate models of the movements of the Sun and Moon.

Can you find...?

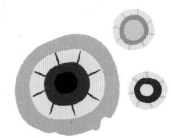

▲Craters
Craters on the Moon are created by the impact of asteroids and other objects from space that have collided with the surface.

▲Satellite
Can you find this satellite in the picture?

Moons

There are 150 known moons in the solar system. They travel around their own parent planet, and all planets and moons travel around the Sun. Only Mercury and Venus have no moons. Jupiter has at least 53, including Ganymede, the largest moon in the solar system. The same side of our Moon always faces us as it travels around the Earth. The dark areas we see are lower and the brighter areas are lunar highlands.

▲Lunar module
Lunar modules were used by astronauts to land on the surface of our Moon.

Can you find...?

People on the Moon

▲Crater
How many craters can you count in this picture?

Only 12 men in history have walked on Earth's Moon. The first successful Moon landing happened on 20 July 1969. Astronauts have since crossed 90 km (56 miles) of its surface.

▲Lunar module
Can you see the lunar module in this picture?

▲Flags
The flags left on the lunar surface have faded and are now completely white.

◄Rock samples
Astronauts on our moon brought back over 400 kg (880 pounds) of rock.

◀Rocket
Can you see this rocket
in the picture?

▲Moon buggy
During the Moon
landings, astronauts
used lunar roving
vehicles or 'moon
buggies' to explore
the Moon's surface.

▼Apollo 11
The Apollo 11
spaceflight was the
first to land men on
the Moon.

◀Astronaut
Can you see the Moon-walking
astronaut in this picture?

15

Can you find...?

Working in space

▲**Spacewalk**
Astronauts sometimes go outside the Space Station to make repairs.

There are now satellites orbiting the Earth where scientists live and work for months at a time. The largest is the International Space Station. It is so big that you can see it in the night sky.

▲**Weightlessness**
There is a near-weightless environment aboard the Space Station.

◀**Experiments**
Experiments in biology, physics and deep space exploration are carried out on the International Space Station.

◀Astronauts
Can you find these astronauts in this picture?

▲Solar panels
There are sheets of solar cells on the outside of the International Space Station. These panels transform solar energy into electricity to power the satellite.

▼Worker
Can you find this astronaut working on the satellite in this picture?

◀Satellite
Can you see the satellite in this picture?

17

Can you find...?

Space probes

▲ **Jupiter**
The Voyager 2 space probe took pictures of Jupiter and its moons as it flew past the planet.

S pace probes are computer-controlled robots that investigate the solar system and deep space. These spacecraft often spend years circling other planets in our solar system and studying them up close with their cameras and scientific instruments. Without them, we wouldn't know much about Jupiter's colourful atmosphere, Saturn's rings, superfast winds on Neptune or the many moons that orbit Jupiter and Saturn.

▲ **Nuclear power**
Satellites that travel beyond Jupiter must rely on nuclear power instead of solar energy from the Sun.

◀ **Mars rovers**
Four 'rovers' have been landed on Mars. They can move around and examine large areas of the planet's surface.

◀Camera

The cameras on the Mars rovers take pictures of the surface so scientists can study its colour, texture and contents.

▲Flyby

Space probes orbit planets and collect information about their atmospheres and surfaces.

▲Crater

How many craters can you count in this picture?

▲Moons

Can you find one of Jupiter's many moons in this picture?

▶ ...anders

...er space probes can send
...ctures of the planet and
...nine soil samples.

Timeline

13.8 billion years ago
The Big Bang occurs and the universe comes into existence.

1942
The first German V2 rocket is launched 100 km (62 miles) from the Earth's surface (the edge of space). The age of space exploration begins.

5 billion years ago
Our solar system is first formed at this time. The Earth formed 4.6 billion years ago.

12 April, 1961
Yuri Gagarin becomes
the first man in space. He
completed one orbit of the
Earth in his spacecraft,
Vostok 1.

4 October, 1957
Russia launches the
first ever satellite,
Sputnik 1, into space.

20 July, 1969
US astronauts Buzz Aldrin
and Neil Armstrong
become the first men to
walk on the Moon.

21

Quiz

1. What is the name of the galaxy we live in?

2. What are asteroids made of?

3. Approximately how much of Earth's surface is covered in water?

4. Who discovered the planet Uranus?

5. Which two planets in our solar system do not have moons?

6. Which spaceflight was the first to land men on the Moon in 1969?

7. What is the largest manned satellite orbiting the Earth?

8. What space probe took pictures of Jupiter as it flew past?

9. What was the name of the first satellite ever launched into space?

10. Who was the first man in space?

Answers:

1. The Milky Way
2. Rock and metal
3. Three-quarters
4. William Herschel
5. Mercury and Venus
6. Apollo 11
7. International Space Station
8. Voyager 2
9. Sputnik 1
10. Yuri Gagarin

Glossary

Asteroid An irregular-shaped rocky body that orbits the Sun.

Atmosphere The layer of gas surrounding a planet or moon.

Comet A ball of rock, ice and dust that produces a visible tail if it travels close to the Sun.

Crater A round hollow on the surface of a planet or moon.

Gravity A pulling force that holds everything together; stars in a galaxy, planets around a star and objects on Earth.

Moon A rocky satellite that orbits a planet.

Orbit The path a planet or comet takes around the Sun, and the path a moon takes around a planet.

Planet A body of rock, or rock and gas, orbiting a star.

Satellite A man-made instrument like a telescope that orbits the Earth, or a moon orbiting a planet.

Solar energy Energy from the Sun, used to produce electricity and to power machines.

Star A spinning ball of hot, luminous gas.

Index

A
Armstrong, Neil 21
asteroids 6, 7, 13, 23

B
Big Bang 20

C
comets 7, 23
constellations 10

E
Earth 4, 5, 6, 7, 9, 10, 13, 14, 16, 20, 21, 23

G
Gagarin, Yuri 21

H
Herschel, William 10
Hipparchus 11

J
Jupiter 6, 13, 18, 19

M
Mars 18, 19
Mayans 11
Mercury 6, 13
moons 4, 7, 11, 13, 14, 15, 18, 19, 21, 23

N
Neptune 18

P
probes 18, 19

S
satellites 9, 10, 13, 16, 17, 18, 21, 23

Saturn 18
solar system 5, 6, 7, 13, 18, 20
space stations 16, 17
Sun 6, 7, 11, 13, 18, 23

T
telescopes 10, 11, 23

V
Venus 6, 13